D/S
MINDFULNESS
JOURNAL

WORD A WEEK FOCUS

WELCOME!

PERSONAL EXPLORATION, AND THE USE OF CLEAR LANGUAGE, IS AN IMPORTANT PART OF GROWTH FOR BOTH A DOMINANT AND A SUBMISSIVE. AS A PERSON EXPLORING AN ALTERNATIVE LIFESTYLE, IT IS IMPORTANT THAT ALL PARTIES ARE ABLE TO EXPRESS THEIR NEEDS, WANTS AND DESIRES.

TO ACHIEVE THIS LOFTY GOAL ONE MUST KNOW WHAT THEY ARE WITHIN SELF.

THIS JOURNAL IS BUT ONE TOOL IN THE ARSONAL YOU WILL BUILD AS YOU EXPLORE D/S RELATIONSHIP. IT CAN BE USED AS A PERSONAL JOURNAL, A COUPLES JOURNAL OR A NOTEBOOK FOR INTIMATE DISCUSSION.

IT IS HOPE IT WILL CREATE INSPIRATION, UNDERSTANDING AND EXPLORE OF AREAS IN WHICH ONE MAY NOT OTHER WISE DELVE.

THIS JOUNAL IS NOT SPECIFIC TO EITHER THE DOMINANT OR SUBMISSIVE VIEW POINT. EACH WRITING PROMPTS CAN BE EXPLORED FROM "BOTH SIDES OF THE SLASH".

AREAS OF EXPLORATION:

- WHAT IS THE DEFINITION OF THE WORD?
- FROM THE DEFINITION, HOW DOES IT APPLY TO A PERSONAL VIEW OF DOMINANCE WITHIN A DYNAMIC RELATIONSHIP?
- HOW DOES IT APPLY TO THE PERSONAL VIEW OF SUBMISSION?
- HOW MIGHT THIS WORD BE EXPLAINED TO A PARTNER(S)?
- WHAT ARE WAYS IN WHICH THE WORD IS DEMONSTRATED?
- WHY/WHY NOT IS THIS WORD IMPORTANT WITHIN IN A CURRENT/DESIRED RELATIONSHIP?
- ARE THERE SPECIFIC CHARACTER TRAITS YOU FIND IMPORTANT FOR THIS WORD?

TABLE OF CONTENTS

GRATITUDE 9
DOMINANCE 11
COURTESY 13
HUMILITY 15
ACCEPTANCE 17
LOYALTY 19
TRUST 21
UNDERSTANDING 23
CONTENTMENT 25
PRIDE 27
INTEGRITY 29
SUBMISSION 31
DETERMINATION 33
OBEDIENCE 35
LEADERSHIP 37
CONFIDENCE 39
PUNISHMENT 41
DISCIPLINE 43
ABSOLUTION 45
COMMUNITY 47
HONOR 49
DUTY 51
COMMITMENT 53
CONSISTENCY 55
TOLERANCE 57

TABLE OF CONTENTS(CON'T)

HONESTY 59
CURIOSITY 61
ETHICS 63
ACCOUNTABILITY 65
NEEDS 67
WANTS 69
DESIRES 71
USEFULNESS 73
CREATIVITY 75
DIGNITY 77
RESPECT 79
LISTENING 81
HEARING 83
EMPOWERMENT 85
IMPATIENCE 87
DISRESPECT 89
SACRIFICE 91
PEACE 93
FORGIVENESS 95
REBELLION 97
PURPOSE 99
INSPIRATION 101
BRATTINESS 103
SURRENDER 105
FREEDOM 107
GOALS 109
CELEBRATIONS 111
PERSONAL NOTES & OBSERVATIONS 113

GRATITUDE

DOMINANCE

COURTESY

HUMILITY

ACCEPTANCE

LOYALTY

TRUST

UNDERSTANDING

CONTENTMENT

PRIDE

INTEGRITY

SUBMISSION

_____

_____

_____

_____

_____

_____

_____

_____

_____

_____

_____

_____

_____

_____

_____

_____

_____

_____

_____

_____

_____

_____

_____

_____

DETERMINATION

OBEDIENCE

LEADERSHIP

CONFIDENCE

PUNISHMENT

DISCIPLINE

ABSOLUTION

COMMUNITY

HONOR

DUTY

COMMITMENT

Consistency

TOLERANCE

HONESTY

CURIOSITY

ETHICS

ACCOUNTABILITY

NEEDS

WANTS

DESIRES

USEFULNESS

CREATIVITY

DIGNITY

RESPECT

LISTENING

HEARING

EMPOWERMENT

IMPATIENCE

DISRESPECT

SACRIFICE

PEACE

Forgiveness

Rebellion

PURPOSE

INSPIRATION

BRATTINESS

SURRENDER

FREEDOM

GOALS

CELEBRATIONS

PERSONAL NOTES & OBSERVATIONS